The Power of Following

You don't have to be a leader to change the world.

Freedom Kongvold

The Power of Following
You don't have to be a leader to change the world

Published by Freedom Enterprises
161 Colvin Rd
Dalton, PA 18414

Additional resources are available at
www.thepoweroffollowing.com

Cover Photo: Evan Kongvold at www.evankongvoldphotography.com
Editor: Steph Whitacre
Cover Design: Jess Creatives

Additional author information at www.freedomkongvold.com

ISBN-13: 978-0692683811

To my wife Kelly.

You have always been my greatest encourager. To Follow God and the dreams he gives me.

My love for you is as big as the sky.

Table of Contents

Preface: The Author

Hello. My name is Freedom and I am a Follower!

Although I have spent my entire life being a Follower, I don't excel at it yet. The truth is, I'm not even a run-of-the-mill Follower. I regularly feel the tension between embracing my ability to follow and my desire to be a leader. I have been told my entire life that, in order to become a success, I need to be a leader. However, after years of workshops, books, seminars and infomercials, I am still much better at being a Follower than I am at being a visionary leader.

I am known among my friends for always having the newest, brightest idea. Even as I sit here trying to focus on writing this book, my mind is whirling at 50,000 feet, considering some new ideas I just heard on a podcast about internet possibilities. I have written down lists (seriously, *lists*) of business and product ideas.

At this point, you may be asking, "Why are these ideas only written down and not being implemented?" That's a great question! The simple, straightforward answer is that I'm not wired to be a trail blazing leader, and many of my ideas would require a team to move them off the paper to actionable steps. An idea alone is not the world's next solution. It takes more than just the vision of a leader to make a concept a reality. It takes additional viewpoints and the support of a force of Followers to make things happen.

Yes, I have ideas, energy, passion, foresight, a willingness to study, goals—the list is endless—and I bet you do too. I have the power to bring strong value to a team, even if I am not a visionary leader. In this book, I want to share with you some of my stories and the things I've learned about following. My dream is to provide you with the confidence and preparation to go and become the hero of your story by becoming a high-capacity Follower.

My name is Freedom and I *am* a Follower.

Followers Unite!

"If your friend jumped off a bridge, would you do it too!?"

We have all heard this uttered from our parents' lips at least once in our lives. I've heard it more times than I can count—and rightfully so! My entire life, especially during high school, I have been prone to mischief. There were never any bridges involved (maybe some cliffs) but I understand my mom's concern about who I was following.

But doesn't this platitude sound a little dramatic? After all, there is nothing wrong with being a Follower! The reason parents often see danger in being a Follower is because the doors to adventure open much faster when you follow someone else. That's why choosing *who* you follow is of utmost importance. I'm confident no parent has ever scolded their child for following the exemplary lead of the disciplined quarterback or the studious captain of the debate team. As a father of four, I would be remiss if I didn't emphasize that there is danger in following the wrong crowd. Be wise when choosing who you follow (we'll talk about this more in Key 4).

Every day, we are bombarded with books, seminars, posters and coffee cups purposed to teach and inspire us to be leaders. However, many of us have no interest or desire to be in charge. Does this mean we need to try harder or just give up, withering away as we wish to become someone else? Of course not! One of life's greatest leadership lessons is to embrace who you are and the power you hold as a Follower. The truth is that the majority of the people you are surrounded by every day are Followers just like you.

Here's the good news:
You don't have to be a leader to change the world!

I'm actually smiling a little as I type this because it sounds absurd in contrast to how most of us were raised. I hope that by the end of this book, you will have this idea firmly planted in your brain. I want you to have the freedom to say, "I'm a Follower," and to be proud of it.

It is natural to gravitate toward Rambo, Jason Bourne, and Steve Jobs-type stories. Many of us even wish to be like them because the idea of being a leader who depends on no one sounds so macho and tough. The way they have conquered the world in a seemingly single-handed fashion is jaw dropping. That's not the reality though.

To start, Rambo and Jason Bourne are fictional characters. Movies are a great place to see heroes or sole survivors take on obstacles and launch movements. Storylines like these connect with the part of us that is tired of injustice. These "one man against the world" stories result in ticket sales; nevertheless, they remain fiction.

On the other hand, Steve Jobs is a real-life example of what we perceive as one man conquering the world. He had fantastic vision and drive, and changed the way we interact with technology, information, and each other. What we can't miss is that while Jobs had strong vision and clear understanding, he did not design, engineer, fabricate, distribute, and sell his game-changing technologies alone. He surrounded himself with teams of people, otherwise known as Followers, who took his visions and turned them into reality. These men and women caught sight of a grand plan and followed Steve Jobs into a future of excellence because he was a man that required nothing less in his ranks.

Just like we see in the revolution of Apple, Followers have changed the world we live in by joining the leadership of others. What does that mean for us and how do we also follow with excellence? That's exactly what this book is about: *how to embrace the Power of Following and become a successful, high-capacity Follower.*

Many of you reading this are wired as visionary leaders, not dedicated Followers. Let me be the first to say, I'm so thankful for you! I'd like to invite you to consider that even the leaders among us should be following someone. If you are a successful leader, you can probably look back at a time in your life when you predominantly played the role of a Follower. I hope this book brings back some memories that make you smile and reinvigorates your desire to follow someone above and beyond where you find yourself today.

In the pages that follow, I am going to share 12 ideas that, when put in action, lay the foundation for a lifetime of following. I call these ideas my Keys to Following. In no way is it an exhaustive list. There are numerous more principles that could be added. These 12 Keys are the ones I have learned through my own trial-and-error experiences and from watching the successes and failures of others. Before we jump in, there are a few things I would like to tell you about the content found in this book.

The first is that *I tell a lot of stories.* Personal stories are one of the best ways to grasp a concept, an experience, and the people around us. I wish I could invite you into my living room and listen as you tell me yours. Some of my stories may sound whacky, but I promise, they are all true.

The second thing you should know about this book is *you will occasionally see references to passages in the Bible.* It's not many, but there are some. I want to point this out now because I know that back in the day, if I were to pick up a book that referenced the Bible, I would put it right back on the shelf. Please don't be like that younger version of me. Still not convinced? Let me tell you a story.

Meeting H.B

About 17 years ago, I met H. B. He was a professional man and probably one of the best-dressed guys I had met up until that time. He was a little over five feet tall and built like a Ford. *Tough.*

I met H. B. during a business seminar held at a restaurant. He was a leader in a multi-level business development program I planned to join. I was looking for a leader to follow that could guide me to greener professional pastures and he and his partners fit the bill. I've always been a skeptical guy and, especially in my younger years, I kept my radar shield up looking for wayward motives. The night I met H. B. was no different.

After the information meeting, I was standing to the side, waiting for my pre-arranged sit down. At this meeting, we were going to go over the details necessary for me to join the team and begin my bright, new future. H. B. was talking to a group within earshot of where I was standing when I heard him say, *"Thank God..."*

My aforementioned radar went off and I thought, "Oh crap, did he really just *thank God* and actually mean it?" I began looking more closely around the room, taking in my surroundings, as my mind raced, *"Wait a minute. Nice, friendly, well-dressed people who say they care about me and are willing to help me succeed."* My inner radar skyrocketed to DEFCON 4, *"Is this a ploy to save my soul instead of to help me get rich!?"* As I waited my turn to speak with H. B., I felt agitated that I had caught him acting with such a shameful motive.

I'm sure that right now you are wondering what on earth was wrong with me. That's a fair question. I had grown up around Christians, and at this time in my young adult life, had decided that Christianity was not for me. After I made the decision that I had no desire to be a Christ follower, it seemed like every churchgoer in the world had come out of the woodwork to apply pressure on me to convert. This only sent me further away and made my radar all the more sensitive. Whether you agree with where I was at during this time of my life or not, it is an important insight for understanding what happened next.

When H. B. finished his conversation with the other guests, he walked over and greeted me warmly, fully expecting my cordial reciprocation. Instead, I blasted him, "I heard you say 'thank God' over there! Let's get something clear. I'm interested in doing business together to make money and learn success, but I *am not* interested in Bible studies or church services!"

I'll never forget the look on his face. H. B. had this way of sincerely smiling even though he was probably thinking, "This guy is an idiot." He looked right at me and simply replied, "What?" I repeated my charge to him and watched him process my perspective. We then had the following exchange:

> *H. B.:* Freedom, are you a football fan?
>
> *Me:* Yes.
>
> *H. B.:* Have you ever seen a football player score a touchdown and celebrate by pointing to the sky or even kneeling in the end zone as a way of thanking God?
>
> *Me:* Yes.
>
> *H. B.:* Are all his teammates who are celebrating with him also believers in God?

Me: No.

H. B.: So is it possible that people with different beliefs can work together as a team, using the same playbook, and moving toward a common goal?

Me: Uh, yes.

H. B.: Great. Let's get started.

My mind was blown! Man, that H. B. had a way about him. I honestly was disappointed that I thought I had caught him being sneaky, but instead was humbled by his wisdom. This would be the first of many lessons I learned from H. B. and the amazing group of leaders in that program.

Since that initial conversation with H. B., I have experienced some changes in my own life. I now believe in God and that the Bible is one of the greatest books ever written on how to live a life of true success. It is packed with wisdom and principles that all of us use regularly, even though we are not always aware of the principles' origins. Whether you lean toward believing like H. B. or siding with young Freedom, I hope you find the Biblical wisdom shared in this book beneficial.

Finally, *the Keys to Following sound simple.* That's because they are! If you're expecting John Maxwell or Dale Carnegie level wisdom, you better put this puppy down. Men like Maxwell and Carnegie are leaders of leaders, and I am not one of them. What I will promise is short chapters with easy-to-apply truth. In these pages, you will find material you can use tomorrow without needing a degree or certification. You won't even need a dictionary by your side in order to absorb the content.

Most of us are not visionary leaders. Yet we do have the ability to make a big impact. Let's move forward together.

Are you ready to unleash your power as a Follower?

Key 1: Commit To Your Role

There I was, hanging from a steel beam. This wasn't just any ole' beam like the kind that gets repurposed as a chin-up bar in a home basement. No, this metal bar had an important purpose. It was positioned to keep boats from drifting off the edge of the lake and into the abyss below. The abyss of which I speak plummeted hundreds of feet before shooting under a dam that produced electricity for the neighboring town. My feet were dangling over this watery gap in the surface of the earth, my fingers gripping the slippery, wet beam.

I clearly remember being 100 percent scared and freaked out that night. It was late and I was with some friends. One member of our group was known for being a little more adventurous than the rest of us. Don't get me wrong, we were *all* adventure seekers, but this particular friend always had a way of pushing us a bit further. He had a way of leading us into danger with a smile on his face. He had the kind of grin that made us feel like whatever he proposed was a great idea.

As I hung there watching the water of the lake flow toward me at eye-level before crashing with deafening noise right beneath my feet, I had a revelation. I suddenly knew this foolish trick was something I absolutely would *never* have done on my own. Regaining strength and ignoring the shaking in my arms, I pulled myself back to a sitting position on the beam and shimmied to safety, vowing I would *never* do something like it again. On that night, I had followed someone far more insane than me and he had led me somewhere I still can't believe I went.

While this story is an excellent example of the Power of Following, I'd be the first to tell you to never do what I did that night. Due to daring individuals with persuasive leadership skills like my friend, being a Follower is often frowned upon. In a culture that emphasizes individuality, people often question why you would follow another person and risk security when you can pave your own course.

Being a Follower is not a sexy idea. In fact, in some circles, the idea that you can be a Follower *and* be successful is considered ridiculous. If you're reading this book in paperback, you may even feel a compulsion to hide the cover from others. After all, people may ask why someone would want to follow rather than lead?

When we gather at family events or class reunions and begin to engage in the comparison dance, we are quick to measure individual success and happiness in direct correlation to personal leadership responsibilities. We overhear people say things like, *"Well, I led such-and-such a group to double digit growth,"* or, *"I'm in management now."* What we don't often hear is someone declaring, *"I'm pleased to say I've identified a leader and am committed to intentionally following him."* Most of us have never overheard or uttered similar words.

The difficulty is that the message we hear in most marketing and media circles is that, in order to achieve success, we must have a brilliant, history-changing idea, business savvy, and a guerrilla attitude. We are told to focus on conquering the world. All too often we believe the lie that only leaders are valuable. This hits us at our core. Before we know it, a misguided desire to lead might even turn into a pride issue. This is not to say that a desire to lead is self-centered; however, a desire rooted in the wrong motivation might become a challenge. The "Me Monster" comes out when pride is unbridled. It can be tough for one to admit they may be a better Follower than a leader. It's this type of false roadblock that we need to see clearly in order to move past. After all, pride can ruin lives.

Would you rather be a successful Follower or a failed leader?

I'll take success any day. There is nothing wrong with choosing to not be a leader as the world defines it. Consider the business strategy of franchising. This concept is built on following an already blazed path to success so you don't have to hack through unknown territory. Most of the entrepreneurs who jump into the franchise system do so for the specific purpose of following a proven method. These individuals spend time, energy, and financial resources to choose a team of leaders they should follow in setting up their business.

In addition to franchising, there are other common words that carry the connotation of following. These include mentoring, apprenticing, consulting, and advising. Each of these arrangements is a variety of following; they all require submitting to the authority of another person who will lead one to their chosen destination. By stripping away these other names, we can get straight back to the basics and focus our minds on the core act of following. I believe this will awaken our sense of responsibility to make wise decisions regarding who, where, how, and why we follow those we have placed ahead of us.

I recently had a discussion with a relative about who is more important: the leader or the Follower. This is a chicken and the egg scenario. There will always be strong argument for the leader or visionary to be the most important. Without ideas, vision, and someone who knows why we're doing what we're doing, we would be lost. That being said, the Follower also holds an immense amount of power.

A Follower can make or break a movement.

It takes courage to be a Follower. In some cases, it may require more from the follower than the leader. The leader is in charge and knows why he does what he does. The Follower must emulate respect and trust even in the face of uncertainty.

In 1962, social psychologist Solomon Asch was the first to perform an experiment that has been replicated many times since. In his experiment, Asch teamed up with the television show Candid Camera to display the power of one leader on the dynamics of a group. In a replication of this experiment that I saw, the scene opens on a group of people riding in an elevator. After a moment, one of the passengers, who is a plant for the experiment, turns to face the side wall of the elevator instead of looking straight at the doors as usual. At this point, you can imagine the thoughts of the other riders.

"Is he *crazy?"*
"Why is he *doing that?"*
"That person is very odd."
"Does he *know what* he *is doing?"*

The next part is what fascinates me. After a few moments, another participant turns to face the same side wall as the first Follower. You can see on the faces of those who remain facing the typical direction that their thoughts have shifted from the strange individual to themselves.

"Am I *missing something?"*
"What's going on that I *don't know about?"*
"I don't want to be different! Should I *turn to the side too?"*

Without speaking a word, the others in the elevator, one by one, slowly begin to turn to the side. What we see from this experiment is that it takes one person (the leader) to get things rolling, but the first Follower is significant. They can enact change simply by following. In a large group setting, each additional Follower has the power to accomplish more than was possible before. We've all seen this in our own lives, in meetings at work or within our friend group. One person throws out an idea that everyone winces at, but as soon as a second person says they agree, the attitude of the group begins to change. Forward motion is made.

The world needs people who strive to be thoughtful, strategic leaders. We also need people who aspire to follow with excellence. We need a force of Followers who are passionate about making an impact in their own lives and in the lives of others. If you feel stalled out, it might be time for you to find a trailblazing leader who will help you pass through doors and seek adventures you wouldn't reach on your own. The responsibility is on you. You get to decide.

As you continue to the next Key of Following, I encourage you to release your hesitations that might be motivated by pride or fear, and step into the world of following. After all, the Power of Following is right outside your door waiting for you.

Questions to Unlock

1. Are you willing to submit to the advice, suggestions or authority of another person? *If not, what are you afraid may happen if you do?*

2. Think of a time you followed someone (a coach, parent, spiritual guide, teacher, etc.). Can you see how your life was changed through this act of following?

3. Is it difficult for you to accept the idea of being a Follower? *If yes, why do you think that is?*

Key 2: Know Where You Want To Go

As I sat across from the man, it was hard to believe this would be my leader. His lips were covered in tuna fish, which spilled out of his mouth, as he buried his face into his sandwich at the mentorship luncheon I was attending. I was a business student, and this was my first meeting with the successful business leader with whom my program had paired me.

The way the man devoured his sandwich with no regard to the tuna dripping down his chin went against everything I understood about etiquette. If my mother had been there, she would have provided a lesson on how to eat correctly, should he ever have the opportunity to eat with the Queen of England. As I processed that this was the leader I was about to follow, I found myself asking one question: *Why?* I still laugh when I think back on this first meeting.

Fortunately, my initial impression of Mr. Tuna was not an accurate indicator of who he truly was as a leader. The first lesson he taught me was that a good mentor can be hidden behind my hasty judgment. Despite outward appearances, he was a good man who knew his trade well and had an excellent reputation. I learned many lessons from him, most importantly that his craft, and my goal to be a stockbroker, was not actually what I desired to do with the rest of my life. I thought I knew where I wanted to go, but after having the opportunity to follow someone ahead of me on the journey, I realized that particular profession was not for me.

Over the course of my year as an apprentice under Mr. Tuna, I was introduced to a myriad of people who came through his office. Many of these people were leaders in their own fields. It was during this time that I met another leader who, within a few short years, became the next person I would follow.

We all come in contact with various types of leaders on a regular basis. It is inevitable that each of us will change our personal course at least once or twice, if not several times. The Power of Following can be unleashed whether change is a rare occasion or if change in your life always seems to be only a sneeze away. When change happens, it is possible that a shift in leadership is right around the corner as well.

If you have a hunger to know how to follow, you must already have a destination in mind. Maybe there is a career path you are eager to pursue, but need help getting started. Or maybe you are interested in volunteering with an organization that is doing work for which you feel passionate, but you want to know the best way to utilize your time and resources. It is also possible that you are already invested as an employee or volunteer, and want the leaders of the company or organization to see you as someone who desires to excel in your role.

It can be difficult to know where you want to go and what knowledge you would like to gain. Spend time with any high school student and you'll quickly be reminded how intimidating it can be to answer the question, "What are you going to do next?" This is what I call a nunchuck-to-the-throat type question. Ask a student too eagerly, and you will be met with a wide-eyed stare. In an attempt to calm future-related anxiety, many of us try to ease the situation by saying, "It's okay. You'll figure it out." I always chuckle when I overhear this type of exchange because many of us are still trying to "figure it out" as well!

What would your response be if someone were to walk up to you right now, look you in the eyes, and ask in a caring voice, "What do you want to do with your life?" We all have ideas, suggestions, and thoughts about our general direction, but it feels impossible to know for sure. This question will follow us throughout our entire lives as we continually evaluate our progress and what brings us the most happiness. In our youth, we start out with the attitude of blazing our own way and not letting "the man" tell us what to do. As we follow this path, many of us hope someone will come alongside us and provide guidance because going at it alone is not working out as well as we anticipated.

One Sunday morning, I was filling my car at the gas station. I somehow fell into conversation with the gentleman pumping gas on the other side of the pump. It didn't take long before we were talking about our kids, hobbies, and work. He told me a great story that had taken place in his life about ten years prior.

After years of success in the HVAC business, his wife came to him one day and asked a powerful question, "If you could do anything for a career, what would it be?" Whoa. As MC Hammer once said, "It's Hammertime!"

I love that she was willing to ask this question during a time when they were financially stable and content. Her query wasn't motivated by impending failure or a need for change. She simply wanted to take a moment to stop and think about the possibilities.

My new friend's response to his wife's question was equally fantastic in its honesty. He looked her in the eye and said, "I don't know." This is so relatable. For many of us, myself included, we just don't know.

The man continued his story by saying that his wife caused him to begin thinking about the future like he never had before. After about a week, he went back to her and announced that he had it all figured out—he knew what they were going to do with the rest of their lives! He laid out his plan to quit HVAC work, sell everything, and move south to the beach. Once they were there, they would sell and rent beach umbrellas during the tourist season and take the rest of the year off.

As you can imagine, telling his wife that he planned to leave a successful career to go sell beach umbrellas didn't land well. He asked her to think about it. After a moment of consideration, she fired back, "You're crazy, find something else!" I laughed when he told me this— it's real life and I love it! After doing some more thinking and research, my friend ended up deciding to establish a crane rental business. Today he and his wife own a successful company renting cranes. This business allows his family the opportunity for greater success than the HVAC industry had permitted.

Even though this story is not about following, it is a real-life example of the importance of taking the time to decide where you want to go. It's obvious we need to spend some time focused on setting the compass in the right direction. Here are three settings to help navigate you forward. We'll begin with happiness and then explore passion and success.

Happiness.

What a word. Happiness means *to be in a state of well-being and contentment.* Sounds like a dream, doesn't it! I would bet top dollar that whatever it is you are chasing, you believe it will make you happier. This is a common goal for all of us. Nobody spends time strategizing how to make his or her life worse. Even those of us who have made critical errors have done so with the belief that whatever we were doing would make us happier at least in the moment.

When we look at life through the lens of happiness, it is important not to focus on a quick fix or a temporary patch. Take a moment to look at what a full picture of happiness would look like for you. Consider what your life would look like framed in a mindset of true contentment. Think about what would be different in terms of your finances, career, health, faith, family relationships, and level of fulfillment. As you think this over, write it down. If this is all the paper you've got, jot your thoughts in the margins of this book.

Having your happiness setting dialed in and having a clear definition on paper will help you stay on course as you locate a leader to follow. Once you know where you want to go, you can start looking for the right person to take you there.

Passion.

What makes you feel fired up? What possibilities get you excited? What charges your battery when you have an opportunity to get your hands on it? The answer to these questions will reveal something about your passions. Passion, when recognized and used correctly, is an amazing force. It heals wounds and gives us skin of titanium. It quiets the voices of hecklers and gives us the momentum to push past our limits. When we figure out what stirs our passionate side, we can truly think about where we would go if we disengaged our internal brakes and were truly willing to follow someone into unknown territory or even battle.

I was recently listening to a podcast by Andy Stanley, who I believe to be one of the greatest leaders today. In the podcast, Stanley asks, **"What breaks your heart?"** When you look around you, what is it that rips your heart apart? What is the problem for which you are willing to do almost anything in order to be part of the solution? Passion lives in places like that.

One of my favorite depictions of passion is Mel Gibson's character in the movie *Braveheart*. Just saying the name "William Wallace" brings a colorful image to mind. His heart broke over the oppression under which his family and countrymen lived. His passion welled-up from the knowledge that he could make a difference and be part of the solution.

I have two friends who, when they began dating, were both managers at big-box retail stores. When I first met them, they were both hungry to climb the corporate ladder. For this reason, they worked long hours, and had never spent Christmas or any other major holidays together. They lived their lives like passing ships.

As my friends spent more time together and with our group of friends, they realized that their relationship and time together was more important than anything they could achieve in the workplace. They made the decision that one of them would quit the rat race. Soon after, they were married. As their relationship grew and ability to communicate improved, it became evident that they were not as passionate about achieving in the corporate world as they once thought. Their hearts and minds were awakened to a passion for caring for children. They opened their home to the foster care system and have welcomed through their door a steady stream of children who need loving arms wrapped around them. They have loved these children and provided guidance to many. My friends discovered happiness by finding what is their true passion.

**If you can identify your true passion,
you will achieve more.**

All great leaders have the desire for their Followers to be passionately engaged in their mission. Knowing what you are passionate about will reveal where you want to go and, ultimately, who to follow.

Success.

We all desire to be successful. If you put a group of young boys around a campfire, eventually a challenge will begin to hit a target with a rock or to jump over the fire. Actually, this isn't limited to young boys—grown men do the same thing! We have an innate desire to find something to do and to be successful at it.

Success can mean many things. It can mean the attainment of popularity or profit. It can mean the achievement of prosperity. Or it can be the accomplishment of a goal or purpose. Clarifying how you define success is important because there is no way to reach it without knowing what it means to you. You may focus your success on how you raise your children or on being a tremendous spouse. You may look for it in a career as an entrepreneur. You may seek to be the best volunteer ever.

A few years ago, I took on a volunteer role at an organization that has an impact on the lives of many. One of the first questions I asked leadership was, "What can I do to be successful in this role and fill this position with excellence?" The answer I received was to read whatever I could in regard to the subject matter and to listen to related podcasts. The more information I could soak in, the more value I could bring to help the leaders attain their vision. If you don't know what success looks like in your specific pursuit, seek out the wisdom of those who do. It is critical to define what success looks like to you. Although you should seek the input of others, only you can choose the final definition. It's yours to chase.

I hope these three areas—happiness, passion and success—cause you to think. If success is what you are focused on, you'll need to dig deeper to define what it looks like. The same is true of happiness and passion. The real answers to what you are looking for may be several layers down. Here is an example of what I mean:

Question:	What are you focused on?
Answer:	I'm focused on attaining success.
Question:	Success in what area?
Answer:	Leading my family.
Question:	How would you define achieving success in leading your family?

Answer:	Having successfully earned my family's trust in my authority, knowing that all members know how much they are loved and cherished, seeing my children make wise choices on their own, etc.
Question:	Do you currently have the knowledge to attain your goal?
Answer:	Some, but not as much as needed.

This string of questions pushes deeper into what is needed to get from point A to point B. In the above example, there is awareness of a lack of knowledge. The next step would be to identify where additional knowledge can be found and what leaders you could choose to follow. The Power of Following can only be unlocked once your destination has been set.

The act of even *locating* where you want to go is a journey in and of itself. Your path to this discovery will probably look different than mine and from the person sitting next to you. However, it should revolve around what makes you happy, the things for which you are passionate, and your definition of success. Set your course and go.

Questions to Unlock

1. Looking around you right now, what would you like to change in your life? Where would you like to go?

2. What do you foresee as the outcome brought about by this change or destination?

3. Do you currently have access to the knowledge necessary to make this change a reality? *If not, whom should you contact or what resource should you obtain?*

Key 3: Surround Yourself with Wise Mentors

In the late 1990s, my wife and I spent a few years on the fast moving train of network marketing. Looking back, it was one of the greatest things we've ever done. As a young, financially strapped couple, we learned so much from being surrounded by people who had dreams, goals, and a desire to better themselves. The lasting impact of those years came from two main sources: *reading books* and *spending time with experienced people.*

During this period of our lives, we began to read in pursuit of growth, rather than as just an entertaining hobby. We picked up books on goals, relationships, communication, marriage, and whatever other topics our mentors recommended to be helpful. In fact, this was one of the first times in my life that I would sit and read the Bible, in search of the success principles I had heard were in there.

Words hold a special power

The more books we read, the more our outlook shifted on life and affected our decision-making and relationships.

In addition to widening our circle of influence through the books we read, my wife and I also surrounded ourselves with leaders within our business model. As we followed them toward financial success, their care for others, dedication to their spouses, and other character traits began to rub off on us. To this day, I can see the positive impact they left on our family.

The result of these friendships was drastically different from the friendship I told you about earlier that led me to dangle from a slippery beam directly above a dam. Notice that I use the word *result*. The results of following each group were dramatically different, but how I got to each place was the same. I arrived at both of those places by choosing to follow.

To most of us, the idea that the books you read and the people you spend time with will influence your life is not a new principle. It's like if I told you that exercise and eating properly is the best way to lose weight and be healthy. We all *know* that this is true.

We also know that it results in feeling better about ourselves and having more energy. But for some reason, we like to skip the simple ideas of diet and exercise and complicate our health by making it a riddle. Billions of dollars are spent on seminars, weird fitness tools (remember the machine that was just a towel wrapped around your backside that supposedly would shake you into shape!?), and magic pills, when all you really need to know is to eat correctly and exercise regularly.

Just like diet and exercise are the key components of good health, the equation for finding success as a Follower is equally simple:

You will become like the people you follow and the books that you read.

If this were a comic book, this is where you would see the big bubble that says, "KA-POW!" There is so much power in this simple sentence. You see, we can't help but be affected by the things we put into our heads. Our brains adapt the information we hear—factual or not—as truth. Our thoughts will lead us somewhere, making it critical for us to choose inputs that will lead us to a purposefully chosen destination.

If you don't believe that our brains view the information we receive as truth, consider the following examples. Think about a time you or someone you know was playing a video game in your living room. You were looking at a flat screen, rendering a pixelated world with seemingly no connection to reality. Then an overall-clad, mustachioed Mario comes on the screen and you begin moving the controller, literally jumping out of your seat as you make him jump on screen. Or consider how we react to horror movies. Everyone knows that the images are fabricated and not real, yet our hearts race and our eyes widen in response to the stories that unfold on screen. Our minds cannot differentiate between reality and fiction.

We need to be vigilant in protecting the ideas and images that we put in our heads. If we believe this strongly enough to guide our children on who they allow to influence their lives and what images they put in their heads, why wouldn't we do the same for ourselves?

The Power of Following will be unleashed regardless of who you follow

Who you surround yourself with can lead you to prison or to paradise. You are responsible for choosing the leader you align with and the direction you head. If you are following a leader on faith and reading their recommended materials, you must do your due diligence to ensure you aren't hitching yourself to the wrong train.

If you are in high school or college, I want to say how thrilled I am that you are taking charge of your life from a young age. You have set yourself apart from the pack just by taking the time to learn more about how you can follow with excellence. I'd like to encourage you to continue taking responsibility for yourself and not depend on the mandate of a parent or coach to prod you in being smart about who you hang out with.

There may be some confusion regarding the difference between someone who cares about you versus someone who can lead you forward. You probably have friends and family members who would never intentionally hurt you or purposely lead you in the wrong direction. However, this does not mean they are the best people to ask for guidance. They may not know the strategy necessary to lead you toward your goals, but they still hold the place of highest value in your life. Surround yourself with wise leaders and mentors, but do so in a way that is balanced and honors your primary relationships.

In summary, decide carefully what materials you read. I add podcasts, blogs, and other tremendous sources of information to this list. We live in a time of unlimited access to ideas and information. Whether you have an hour a week or ten hours a week to absorb content, make it a priority to learn from the ideas of others.

In addition to absorbing new content on the topic you are pursuing, surround yourself with leaders in that field. It might be the leader of the nonprofit where you volunteer or a mentor from the church you attend. This person doesn't have to be your best friend or closest confidant. The key is observing closely how this individual interacts with the world around them and asking the question of how you can do what you do better.

Questions to Unlock

1. Think back over the last twelve months. Who did you spend the most time with?

2. Are the people you spend the most time with helpful or harmful in guiding you to your destination?

3. Identify an individual who has made an impact as a leader in your life. What makes this person impactful?

4. What books, podcasts, blogs, etc. do you read and listen to the most?

Key 4: Find a Leader to Follow

"A disciple is not above his teacher, but everyone when he is fully trained will be like his teacher." – Luke 6:40, ESV

As a teenager, I had my eyes set on making millions. Even though I was young, I knew I needed to find someone to teach me how to achieve this goal. Some of you may laugh, but at an early age, I made up my mind that Donald Trump was my key to making it big. For all of you Millennials, this might sound confusing. But Trump used to be known for something other than firing people on television, running for president, and his iconic hair. In the 1980s, Trump was known for making millions in the real estate business through savvy negotiating skills and cutthroat business gumption.

For this reason, when I was 12 or 13 years old, I began to do two things every single year. The first thing I did was buy the J. K. Lasser tax guide for the current year and read it, absorbing what I could about tax strategy. The second was to send a letter to Donald Trump. In these letters, I would proclaim my desire to be successful and my confidence that, if he would only give me a chance, I would be a tremendous asset as his apprentice (keep in mind, this was before he actually had a show titled *The Apprentice)*. Who could argue with my logic! Well, Trump sure couldn't. And he didn't. In fact, I don't think that in the ten straight years I sent these letters, even one of them made it past his gatekeeper's desk.

I clearly remember the final year I wrote a letter to Trump. I was simultaneously filling out the application to appear on the first season of his soon to be hit show *The Apprentice.* I was married and had young children. As I filled out the application, I struggled with the idea that, if chosen, I'd be required to spend several months away from my family. My desire to be wealthy was still intact, but my core values had changed. I now had a desire to learn from a leader who understood business success, but would also guide me in how to be a great husband and father. It was a strange moment.

After all those years of feeding a burning desire for prosperity at all costs, I was waffling! I threw away the half-filled application and the letter I had written. The point on my navigational compass had moved and I needed a new leader to follow.

No matter what area of life you would like to improve, there is a leader to follow. There is someone who sets the pace and exudes confidence in the area in which you would like to grow. Part of embracing the life of a successful Follower is vetting leaders to find the one who you will follow.

In the movie *American President,* there's a quote that perfectly summarizes man's intrinsic thirst to have leadership. Michael J. Fox's character is speaking to the president, played by Michael Douglas, and implores him to step up:

> People want leadership, Mr. President, and in the absence of genuine leadership, they'll listen to anyone who steps up to the microphone. They want leadership. They're so thirsty for it they'll crawl through the desert toward a mirage, and when they discover there's no water, they'll drink the sand.

We all desire leadership

Even when it is hard for us to say we are being Followers, leadership is what we crave. The strength of this desire is why we need to exhibit intelligence and be proactive in choosing who we follow. When evaluating leadership, there are strong identifying traits for which we can look. They're not things like being the best dressed, driving a fancy car or having great hair. They are traits that dig deeper into the character of the individual. When identifying someone to follow, here are some traits to look for:

Passion and Attitude.

Learning what a person cares about is a great place to start. Obviously, if the individual's passion is in real estate and yours is in the clothing business, he may not be the most beneficial leader for you to follow. You may like him as a person and he may have an excellent reputation, but if his passion does not align with yours, continue your search. Once you find a leader whose passions align with your own, observe how he overcomes obstacles. Consider if he is equipped with a mindset that can lead others to the goal despite challenges.

Visible Successes.

In an era of social media and Photoshop, identifying true success can be difficult. However, it is important to seek the wisdom of someone who is thriving in his or her realm of expertise. When one of my sons expressed a desire to enter the media production field after high school, we didn't sit down with the school's guidance counselor who is an expert on college applications and academic scholarships. Instead, we went on a road trip to meet with individuals who have found success in the production industry. In the end, we saved over $100,000 in school bills and a whole lot of time. The point is, look for those who know their stuff and not just those who have an opinion.

Failures and Shortcomings.

Observing how someone handles failures and shortcomings will tell you a great deal about their commitment to honesty and humility. Before you align yourself with a leader, you should feel comfortable with their level of honesty and ability to talk about mistakes. Another reason that failure is important is because it reveals a great deal about how a leader handles adversity. This shows a commitment to leading through challenges; keep in mind, if challenges aren't happening, then it is possible nobody is leading. The important thing to evaluate is if challenges and failures are being overcome or if the leader is continually stuck in the same rut. Look for a person making forward motion.

Circle of Influence.

This goes back to our earlier conversation about books and people. If you want to learn more about a leader, consider the books they are reading and who they surrounded themselves with and who they choose as trusted friends and advisors. Even strong leaders are not immune to the influence of others and it is important to observe who your leader places in high regard.

Genuine Concern for Others.

Good leaders have been taught that Followers aren't as impressed by how much a leader knows as they are by how much a leader cares. It's easier to take advice from someone who has your best interest in mind, as opposed to someone who spits out facts and information without considering your story. That being said, it is possible to experience the care of a leader without having a personal relationship with him or her.

Two leaders who come to mind as examples of this are the author John Maxwell and Andy Stanley of North Point Community Church. I have never met either of these guys but, after reading their books and listening to their podcasts, I am certain that they truly care about people. Their style of coming alongside others they desire to help and benefit is a far cry from that of the radio host who brings people on his show to lead them into a train wreck for the purpose of ratings. We can all perceive who has a heart for benefiting others and who is in it for their own advantage and selfish gain.

These traits are a great start to use as a measuring tool for choosing a leader. Keep in mind that nobody is perfect, and if you look for a leader who is without fault, you may wind up disappointed. But that's okay! After all, one of the greatest benefits of following a leader is seeing where other people have stumbled and overcome challenges.

Questions and Challenge to Unlock

1. Make a list of leaders you have had in your life. How do they compare to the list in this chapter?

2. In light of what you learned in this chapter, who would you identify as possible leaders in your life?

3. This week, reach out to at least one of these people and ask to meet for coffee. Discuss your desired destination and ask if they will help lead you there.

Key 5: Lift Others Up

Last night, I was with a group of friends, and two questions came up that sparked a great conversation. The first question was, "What great life lessons did you learn from your parents?" and the second was, "Who made an impact in your life while you were growing up?" We went around the circle and each friend provided a short history and explanation of his answer.

One of the lessons I clearly remember my mom teaching me took place when I was a young teenager. I was 13 years old, and my mother, younger siblings, and I were moving from our home to another apartment two blocks away. We had no moving van, pickup truck, or other means to haul large objects. We had to either load our small car and drive the two blocks or walk back and forth with our arms full of our possessions. As you can imagine, this was tedious, exhausting, and drew a lot of attention from the neighbors who watched us traverse the short route over and over again.

After numerous trips, our arms and legs felt like jelly. We had moved everything out of the apartment except the large appliances. Standing in the kitchen, staring down the large refrigerator, I felt as though I had reached my limit. As we began a futile attempt to lift the monstrosity, I could not handle the weight and began to whine and complain. I told my mother that moving the hunk of metal two blocks was impossible.

In that moment, I learned from my mother that a leader is not someone easily deterred. She nipped my whining in the bud and said words that changed me forever. With authority in her voice, she said,

"Freedom, we *have* to move this refrigerator. There is no choice. We have nobody to help us— it's just you and me, and we *will* move it."

Wow! The lesson my mom taught me was the power and confidence that comes when one stops attempting and starts doing. To this day I have no idea how, but we moved that refrigerator the two blocks.

While my mother's refrigerator lesson was one of strength and determination, a common thread I noticed in many of my friends' stories was that the lessons they learned were the result of observing a leader's failure as often as it was seeing success. I'm sure you can relate to this as well. It seems that sometimes our greatest lessons come from seeing what *not* to do, as much as they are derived from seeing what *to* do.

Let's be honest, we all know there is nobody on earth who is a perfect leader. Unfortunately, social media and a growing number of news networks have increased our ability to focus our attention on the failures of others. Sometimes it seems as though the Followers among us gain more satisfaction from belittling and criticizing the innovators among us, than we do from building up and supporting the achievements of our leaders.

The story I just told you about my mother is an example of a positive lesson she taught me. That doesn't mean that everything she did was of exceptional leadership quality. Like all parents, she made plenty of mistakes. Yet I don't diminish the value of the lessons I learned from her because of the mistakes she occasionally made along the way.

As we choose a leader to follow, we need to constantly keep in mind that perfection will not happen.

There's a reason that bookstores have row after row of books on building leadership skills—because leaders are constantly fine-tuning their approach to getting their Followers to the next level. Part of our role as Followers is to cheer them on in their growth, not tear them down. Showing emotion or having a bad week are not reasons to tear another person apart. In these moments, remind yourself that leaders are human and mistakes sometimes occur. In fact, watching how a leader handles his or her missteps will give you valuable insight into the individual's sense of identity and character.

All great relationships, including that of Follower and leader, contain edification.

Edification is the act of building someone up.

In the context of this conversation, *edification is the moral and intellectual encouragement of leaders in your life*. In Galatians 6:6, Paul tells us, "Let the one who is taught the word share all good things with the one who teaches." The building up of another person can happen through words of affirmation and support. As we see in Galatians, it can also happen when those who are in a position of learning share their newly gained knowledge and successes with those who lead.

For many of us, it may feel like a challenge to intentionally build up another person. The reason this tension often exists is because we live in a world focused on survival. We falsely believe that if we want to be successful, we need to be talking ourselves up. This sounds selfish, doesn't it? Sadly, it's a fact. Without realizing it, our pride can stand in the way of accomplishing so many great things, including the edification of our leaders. In a world that is increasingly self-centric, it is crucial that we identify the attributes and positive qualities of those around us and celebrate them.

It's important to remember that *leaders are people too.* This may sound silly, but seriously, leaders need affirmation and support just like everyone else. If you have ever had someone speak complimentarily of you to others, you understand the feeling of invincibility that these types of words can give. On the flip side, many of us can also remember times when we were in need of encouragement that was not offered. This type of unfulfilled void can create a desert experience, making a leader feel parched and without fuel to move on. If you are choosing to follow someone and are committed to him or her leading you to a desired destination, I hope you agree that it is wise to do what you can to motivate forward motion.

There is also the idea of *trickle-down authority* as it pertains to being a Follower. Many of us fulfilling our roles as Followers are working in environments where personal credibility has not yet been built. As you follow your leader, it is important you speak in a way publicly that makes others enthusiastic about that leader's accomplishments and abilities. In turn, this builds trust between you and the leader, as he sees that you have his best interest in mind.

Imagine you and your leader attend a meeting with a group from another company. In this scenario, the group knows you, but does not know the leader you are introducing to them. Your role is to edify your leader by portraying how and why you know he has the ability to help the group. This is a powerful move as you use your relationship with them to give your leader their attention. By introducing them to your leader, you are also aligning yourself with that person. You have the power to bring credibility to those who you follow. As your leader engages with the group in the meeting, a rapport has been built between you. When the leader says that you are knowledgeable, the group will believe it.

The power of trickle-down authority comes when the leader leaves the room, and the group now looks to you as being *as capable* as the leader you are following!

Setting aside any expectations of perfection and instead edifying the leaders in your life is not only good for the leader but beneficial for you as well. It is amazing what can take place in our own hearts and relationships when we set aside our own agenda and look to the needs of others. My hope is that you see this clearly and begin to implement this principle today.

Challenges to Unlock

1. Think of and write down the names of the leaders you are currently following or have followed in the past. Next to their names, jot down a few of the strengths they display.

2. This week, take a moment to write a note or tell a leader face-to-face about the specific strengths you see in that person and why you appreciate him or her.

Key 6: Be Easy to Lead

When I was 17 years old, I spent a week in Florida. Sure, plenty of people travel to Florida for vacation or to visit family. However, my trip was not planned and I knew none of the details of my visit at the time of departure. I was living in northeast Pennsylvania, and was on my two-mile hike home from work on a Friday afternoon, when a couple friends pulled alongside me in a car. They had an important question to ask.

They said, "Hey, we're taking off tonight for Florida. We have some jobs lined up there. Wanna come?" Not even stopping to think, I responded, "Sure! I just need to grab some clothes and I'm ready." I jumped in the car and they drove me back to the apartment I lived in with my mom and siblings. I walked inside, said hello to my mom, grabbed a few articles of clothing, and went back out to my friend's car.

A journey like this would be an adventure for any group of 17 year-old kids, but we were in for a little extra excitement. We weren't that far down the road when we realized that the car we were driving was using more oil than gas. This problem made it necessary to stop to refill the oil even more frequently than we needed fuel. Being a bunch of high school students, money was tight, and there was no warning that we needed to leave room for oil in our already small budget.

We limped all the way from Pennsylvania to Georgia. Somewhere in the Peach State, I don't remember where exactly, the engine in our car finally blew. Without enough money to fix it, my friend who owned the car turned the vehicle over to a garage in exchange for towing services. What should have been a 14-hour drive to Jacksonville, Florida, where sunshine and jobs awaited us, turned into a three-day haul.

Leaving our disabled car behind at the garage, the group of us continued our trek south on foot. We had been walking for quite some time when a group of locals pulled up and invited us to hang out with them. Of course we agreed, since this meant food and a chance to rest. After sleeping that night in a cheap motel room, we decided to spend the last of our money on bus tickets. We weren't afraid to empty our pockets since, as you remember, my buddy had promised he had high-paying construction jobs lined up for us.

We arrived in Jacksonville just before sunset on Sunday. We had no money and nowhere to sleep, but the air was warm and the beautiful ocean extended in front of us. With few options of places to lay our heads, we decided it would be a great idea to sleep on the beach with the waves crashing at our feet. The only problem with this plan was that the Jacksonville Police Department did not agree that it was a great idea, and we were asked to leave. Two strangers on the beach overheard our conversation with the police and offered us a place to stay for the night. With no other options available, we accepted.

Finally Monday morning came, and we woke up early, excited to connect with our friend's contact who had arranged our jobs in Jacksonville. As my friend silently hung up the phone, we realized that he truly did know a guy, but that there were, in fact, no jobs waiting for us.

There we were, seven states away from our parents, with no car, no money, no contacts, and no place to sleep. It was time to go home, but we had no idea how we would get there. It took several more days and a list of crazy stories before we would found ourselves back in Pennsylvania.

Those seven days of wandering, scheming, and bumming for meals and rides is one of the craziest and stupidest things in which I have ever been involved. By the time it was over, we had blown up a car, run out of money, slept outside as though we were homeless, been held in a detention center, and scared our families to death. Looking back on the situation, I can see how it all started with following the wrong crowd and being far too easy to lead.

After a story like that, I bet you are wondering why on earth one of my Keys to Following is *Be Easy to Lead.* Well, to begin with, I assume that you are wiser than the 17-year old version of me. If you have chosen to pick up this book, I'm positive that you have a direction you are headed and a desire to succeed. As Followers, it is important for us to take responsibility for ourselves.

The Bible tells us that our leaders have a responsibility to guide us. In Hebrews 13:17, the author instructs us,

"Obey your leaders and submit to them, for they are keeping watch over your souls... Let them do this with joy and not with groaning, for that would be of no advantage to you."

In short, those we trust to lead us are entrusted to watch over our well-being.

That being the case, we have the duty to choose a leader who will lead us down the correct path and make it easy for them to lead us. When I followed my friend to Florida with the expectation that he would provide me with a job and a place to stay, I chose unwisely. Sure, it was easy for me to follow him at first. But as his leadership faltered, I stopped being easy to lead.

Foundational to the principle of being easy to lead is finding a leader who is easy to follow. I think you would agree that if someone is willing to take the time and effort to care for your well-being and achievement, it makes sense that you would follow in a way that brings joy to the leader. Beginning with the assumption that this is a leader you trust and with whom you identify, here are some ways you can make yourself easy to lead:

Obey and Submit.
Oh boy, those are big ones. But if you have chosen a leader to follow, or even if a leader has been assigned to you, it is paramount you make a focused effort to be humble in submitting to his or her leadership. As we discussed earlier, pride is a destructive force. It's your responsibility to overcome it.

In a situation where a leader has been assigned to you, you may be thinking, "But they don't deserve the respect of my obedience." Let's take a moment to consider the very real possibility that there may be a cycle that needs to be broken. You see, as a leader experiences resistance and disrespect, he may begin to feel that his Followers are against him rather than for him. In turn, the leader may struggle to enjoy the process of leading and his level of care may diminish.

In this situation, someone needs to be the first to break the cycle. The first possibility is that the leader will continue to persevere in the face of your obstinacy. Over time, you may have an "ah-ha!" moment as his or her care for you outshines your stubbornness. The problem with this scenario is that it puts all of the work on the leader, instead of encouraging you to take responsibility for your attitude and actions. The second possibility for how to break the cycle, and the one I recommend, empowers the Follower to make the change. In this scenario, the Follower continues to submit. In the ideal case, leadership notices this undeserved respect in the face of adversity and is motivated to lead well and live up to the trust that has been given.

Choose a Positive Attitude.

I was recently reading an article about a particular leader's hiring strategy, and he shared something I will never forget. He said that during the hiring process, one of the questions he asks himself is, "Would I want to be sitting next to this person on a cross country flight?" This question speaks to the importance of attitude over knowledge.

Leaders would much rather teach an individual who they enjoy spending time with over someone they can't stand to be around. Our attitude can build morale in an organization, fueling great teamwork, or it can destroy what has been developed faster than a lit match to a stack of hay. We need to focus on and take charge of our attitude.

We all have the choice and ability to control our attitudes. Every child who has seen their mother answer the phone in the middle of a tirade knows this to be true. If it is possible to be upbeat and polite to the person on the other end of the phone while giving your children *the look* for rollerblading in the house again, then it is possible to control your attitude and response toward your boss and those with whom you work.

One quick way to adjust your attitude is to eliminate the phrase "I can't" from your vocabulary. Channel your inner Yoda and tell yourself, "There is no try. Only do." Yes, a difficult task may require that you learn new information or request extra time. Next time you are tempted to say something is impossible, consider what it might take to overcome the obstacle and go for it.

Commit to Being Teachable.

Your commitment to an organization or leader is often displayed by your willingness to learn new things. The majority of great leaders are constantly learning and looking for outlets to teach and grow others. If you insist on doing things your own way and never learning new things, then you are not committed to being a Follower. Your commitment to your goal will be reflected in your eagerness to learn.

Be Honest and Trustworthy.

I think most of us would say we are trustworthy people. In fact, a 2014 article in the Telegraph, a United Kingdom newspaper, revealed how trustworthy even the least trustworthy among us believe ourselves to be. The article told of a study performed by The University of Southampton, in which 79 prison inmates were asked if they believe themselves to be honest and trustworthy. The overwhelming majority agreed they were—an even higher rate than those outside prison walls. Amazing!

I'm not saying that all of us are disillusioned. Yet the results of this study should give us pause to look deep inside ourselves and ask, "Am I truly an honest person?" Being a person of character will breed trust and will ultimately open doors for you as a trusted Follower.

Questions and Challenge to Unlock

1. Take a look at the four examples of ways to be easy to lead. How would you grade yourself in each area? In which specific one do you need to improve?
   a. *Obey and Submit*
   b. *Choose a Positive Attitude*
   c. *Commit to Being Teachable*
   d. *Be Honest and Trustworthy*

2. Set aside time with a current leader in your life and ask for their feedback in these areas. Ask for an honest appraisal. Don't ask a friend.

3. What change can you make this week to be a Follower who is more easily led?

Key 7: Be a Medic

For over 20 years, I've had the honor of being married to the most beautiful, loving woman in the world. I am head over heels for Kelly. But something our close friends know to be true is that there are few topics in which my wife and I see eye-to-eye. It's really amazing how two people can view the world so differently, yet compliment one another so perfectly.

Like most married couples, Kelly and I have embarked on a few home remodeling projects over the years. These are times when our differences become clear. Choosing paint colors, flooring, and cabinetry is a true test of our wills. Before long, questions of sanity and colorblindness begin to fly. How couples on HGTV are so calm when doing projects together is a marvel to me. The only explanation is that there must be a lot of editing to the footage for those shows.

Home projects are not the only area in which Kelly and I don't align. Depending on which of us you ask, dry rub ribs are delicious or gross, cats are good or bad, winter is enjoyable or painful, and on and on it goes. With all of these differences, I am grateful that one of the things Kelly and I agree on is how we desire to care for the people God places in our lives. In our marriage and home, we are dedicated to the pursuit of loving others.

Kelly has always been a caring individual—this is one of the reasons I fell in love with her. She invests her time volunteering, cultivating friendships, and providing meals and compassion to families who are going through tough spots. Her love is endless and quite extraordinary. To Kelly, there is no price too high or distance too far for her to decline an opportunity to show someone how much she cares. Over time and with God's grace, I have found that caring for others and having a home with an open door is something I enjoy too.

Sure, there are times when we miss an opportunity because we mess up or because we need to say *no* to one thing in order to say *yes* to something else. However, as a family, we have found that one of the greatest ways to add value to this world is by caring for the hearts of other people. There is power in letting an individual know you see their worth instead of their inadequacy. To live a life with this consciously on your mind changes everything.

"Medic!" We've all seen war movies or been in places when someone yells this crucially important word. You can hear it ringing in your ears. Not only is it important, it's a matter of life and death! Typically in these situations, the one who runs to the rescue is not the general or top dog. Most often, we find that the individual running into the fray is not a leader, but a Follower. This all-important Follower, the medic, brings life to others around him and his leader when needed.

Would you consider yourself someone who is a life giver or a life sucker?

When you think about the people you interact with regularly—at work, at home, at church, in your friend group—how do you think they perceive you? You can be a person who brings a positive energy, quick to point out the good in others, or a person who always has something negative to say. You can be that guy who seems to create problems just to have something to talk about or you can be full of questions that draw out the stories of others in the room. You can keep everyone on edge by being someone who continually tears others down or you can speak life, putting others at ease by speaking highly of the qualities of others.

All of us have times when we are the ones in need of a medic. There are seasons of life when we are in need of care. We all need someone who speaks life into us; a person who looks for the positive. As a Follower, the skill to bring life, energy, and courage to your leader is a powerful tool. Being a medic is another way that Followers are vital to completing the mission of a visionary leader. Without someone to back them up and help push them forward, our leaders would never have a chance at success.

For those of you who are fans of NASCAR or another variety of racing, you are familiar with the technique of drafting. The idea of drafting is that by a car or vehicle coming up right behind another, the air currents have less drag on the lead car and propel it to go faster. This is exactly what it looks like to be a medic and provide life to a leader.

A biblical example of what it looks like to be a medic is found in Exodus 17. In this story, the Israelites are in battle with the Amalekites. God directs Moses to tell the Israelites' leader Joshua that the Israelites will prevail, but in order to do so, he must raise the staff of God in the air throughout the battle. The English Standard Version tells the story this way:

> Whenever Moses held up his hand, Israel prevailed,
> and whenever he lowered his hand, Amalek

> prevailed. But Moses' hands grew weary, so they took a stone and put it under him, and he sat on it, while Aaron and Hur held up his hands, one on one side, and the other on the other side. So his hands were steady until the going down of the sun. And Joshua overwhelmed Amalek and his people with the sword. (Exodus 17:11-13)

Joshua led the Israelites into battle. Moses provided guidance. Aaron and Hur acted as medics.

It's hard to compare our lives to those of heroes in the Bible but this shows that the concept of a medic is heavenly inspired. You may be asking why you should take the time and energy to look for ways to be a medic to your leaders and others around you. While the story of Aaron and Hur is exemplary, what does it mean to us today? Going back to NASCAR and the picture of drafting, it's important to point out that the lead car is not the only one provided benefit. When drafting, the second car also uses less energy than it would alone, and goes faster than would be possible without the support of the lead car. This seems counterintuitive, but it's true.

Let's return to where we started with the example of marriage and family life. From time to time, all husbands have thrown out the phrase , "Happy wife, happy life." Although a cliché, this statement is true and goes both ways. If we take the time to be a medic to our spouses and care for their needs, our life will also be better. A decaying relationship can usually be traced to selfishness of some kind, in which one spouse is putting themselves ahead of the other person.

Recently I was spending time with a friend, who is also a leader I admire, when a gentleman stopped by to seek advice from him. My friend and his guest invited me to join their conversation. I listened intently as the visitor described, in lengthy detail, what was happening to him.

My friend listened with great compassion.

There's something powerful about watching a leader show genuine interest when listening to those who have nothing to offer, but simply need a listening ear. As the monologue came to an end, I leaned in, ready to hear the sage advice my friend was going to offer on what the man should do with the disappointment and challenges he was facing. After a few words of encouragement, the only advice he offered was that the man should look for an opportunity to serve someone else. Being a medic means taking your eyes off of you and focusing on someone else. It brings value to the life of the other person, while simultaneously bringing benefit to the giver.

It takes effort to bring life to others, but the work is worth it because of the way it exponentially benefits the leaders in your life and moves you forward as well. While it might not be as glamorous as being

Joshua, charging into battle, or Moses with his staff lifted, the medic holding up the leader's arms is an integral part of the story. Don't overlook the power you have been given to fill this role.

Questions and Challenge to Unlock

1. Time for an honest assessment. Do you currently require more from others than you give to them?

2. If you require more from others than you give, what fear or hesitation is holding you back from shifting your focus to serving over receiving?

3. This week, look for opportunities to be a medic and encourage the leader(s) you follow. If you have not yet identified a leader, practice on someone else in your life, like a close friend or family member.

Key 8: Take Ownership

I'll never forget this one friend I had when I was a kid. The main reason I will not forget him is because of a very memorable lesson he taught me when we were in 5th grade.

We were in the prime of our mischievous lives, our minds coursing with exciting ideas mixed with a handful of stupidity. We were filled with a continual drip of adventure and adrenaline, causing us to misinterpret what constituted a good idea.

This particular incident took place one afternoon in library class. A group of us were goofing around near the encyclopedias (this was obviously pre-Google), when my friend presented our group with a handful of torpedoes—small, white paper objects filled with gunpowder that make a loud SNAP when thrown against something hard like a wall or floor. Being in the library, it made perfect sense in our pre-pubescent minds that we could create a tremendous racket by slamming the torpedoes between the heavy pages of an encyclopedia. We stood in the quiet, back corner of the library, huddled around the open book, barely able to contain our giddiness.

As we counted down, filled with anticipation, my friend slammed the thick, heavy encyclopedia shut. We learned in that moment that the reason fireworks explode is from the pressure and energy trapped inside that needs to go somewhere and cannot be stopped.

There was a "BOOM!" louder than you can imagine, that echoed not just through the library, but throughout the entire school as well. The force was so powerful that it blew a hole right through the three inch book of knowledge. As we immediately assessed the damage, our little group scattered from the scene of the crime. Moments later, the principal flew through the library doors. Uh oh. We knew someone was going to be in big trouble, and each of us silently worried, "I hope it's not me."

The principal and our teacher cleared us from the library and sent us back to our classroom. That's when the interrogation began. Back then, teachers and school administrators could threaten students with all sorts of consequences. In this situation, they presented us with the possibility of keeping us all night until someone confessed, if that's what it took. As the boys in our group cowered in fear, avoiding eye contact, my friend who had detonated the torpedo raised his hand and solemnly said,

"I did it."

In addition to the visual of a small firework blowing a hole in an encyclopedia, the reason this story sticks out in my mind was because of the bravery my friend displayed in taking responsibility.

He didn't say, "*We* did it," or, "It was *their* idea." He simply stood up and took ownership for his personal actions. Amazing!

In Proverbs 19:3, the author tells us, "When a man's folly brings his way to ruin, his heart rages against the Lord." Let's take a little poetic liberty and expand on this verse. When a foolish man's failings or shortcomings bring him to ruin or stand in his way of success, he gets upset and looks for someone to blame. He may point a finger at his parents, his leaders, or even at God. This is the opposite of taking ownership.

I was recently watching the show Family Feud, and one of the survey questions was, "At what age, according to adults, do children begin to think they know more than their parents?" According to the 100 people surveyed, the most popular response was 12 years old. I laughed when I heard this, remembering that day in the library with my friends. In order to make the transition from childhood to adulthood, we have to be ready to take ownership of our own decisions and actions. Taking ownership of oneself is a sign of maturity.

As a Follower, truly taking ownership means several things.

First, it means you must take responsibility for your own actions.

Yes, the leader you are following will help guide you, but ultimately you need to show up and do the work. Wanting to be successful without taking responsibility for your actions is like praying to win the lottery, but never buying a ticket. Our culture barrages us with the message that it's okay to blame others for our shortcomings, failures or present circumstances. I in no way want to be insensitive to those reading this who have fallen on hard times through no fault of their own. However, I do want to encourage you to evaluate how you affected your situation today and what step you can take to improve your tomorrow.

Another way to take ownership is to look for the areas in which you can be the solution.

Imagine you are walking through the parking lot at your office, heading in to begin your day's work, and you see a piece of discarded trash at the edge of the lot. At this point, one of three things can happen. The first outcome may be that the garbage doesn't trigger any further thought. The parking lot always has a certain amount of trash in it and this day is no different than yesterday. Or maybe your initial thought is, "What a mess. Someone should clean up that litter!" The third outcome—the outcome that characterizes taking ownership—is to walk to the edge of the lot, pick up the trash, and throw it away. No, that garbage didn't belong to you, but you acted as though it did and took care of it. Leaders, and employers, love to see that kind of initiative. Going the extra step to solve a problem shows that you are truly invested in the mission and vision of your company or organization.

Taking ownership also requires initiative, defined as the ability to assess, analyze, and solve situations or problems independently from the prompting of an outside source. I know what you're thinking, "Hold on, that sounds a lot like a quality found in a leader." Ah, you caught me! You are absolutely correct; a great leader must have the drive to initiate action in order to move his or her team forward. However, this characteristic is not exclusive to leaders.

In order to be a great Follower and team player, you need to push yourself to look for opportunities to assess and initiate action. Great leaders look for ways to help their Followers increase in capacity.

If you deny yourself the opportunity to take initiative, you may find that the doors open to you become narrower rather than wider.

The final aspect of taking ownership is a commitment to "make it happen."

This is perseverance at all costs. Remember the story about my mother and me moving the refrigerator from one apartment to another? In that narrative, my mom assessed the situation and came to the conclusion that there was no way the job would be completed if we didn't make it happen ourselves. She looked me in the eye and said, "There is no choice... it's just you and me, and we *will* move it." In that moment, my mother taught me that taking ownership means stepping up and doing what seems impossible when nobody else can.

In your life, you will meet many opportunities to take ownership and prove you have what it takes. Don't get caught whining like I did when my mother tasked me with moving the refrigerator. Embrace the moment and own what has been placed in front of you.

There's a famous story, written in 1899, by a man named Elbert Hubbard. Later known as *A Message to Garcia,* Hubbard's short story loudly resonates our desire for someone to take ownership and get the job done. What follows is an excerpt from *A Message to Garcia* that highlights this idea of initiative:

> You, reader, put this matter to a test: You are sitting now in your office – six clerks are within your call. Summon any one and make this request: "Please look in the encyclopedia and make a brief memorandum for me concerning the life of Corregio."
> Will the clerk quietly say, "Yes, sir," and go do the task? On your life, he will not. He will look at you out of a fishy eye, and ask one or more of the following questions:
>
> > Who was he?
> > Which encyclopedia?
> > Where is the encyclopedia?
> > Was I hired for that?
> > Don't you mean Bismarck?
> > What's the matter with Charlie doing it?
> > Is he dead?
> > Shan't I bring you the book and let you look it up yourself?
> > What do you want to know for?
>
> And I will lay you ten to one that after you have answered the questions, and explained how to find the information, and why you want it, the clerk will go off and get one of the 2 other clerks to help him find Garcia – and then come back and tell you there is no such man.

It's amazing that something written so long ago is still relevant today! Hubbard's classic story reveals the fact that initiative is a rare, yet important, quality among Followers. Taking ownership is a game changer because most people are not willing to do it.

To unlock the Power of Following, you must be willing to take ownership and work through challenges to their completion.

Your ability to buy in to the direction of leadership and see your role in the process is imperative. Without doing this, you will go nowhere. If you have taken the time to define where you want to go, and selected a leader to follow, it is time to take ownership of your part in the adventure.

Questions and Challenge to Unlock

1. Think for a moment of your workplace, volunteer role, or even your relationships. What can you do to show that you are taking ownership of your place on that team?

2. Is there a job or role in your setting that you are unwilling to do (*for example, a menial task like taking out the trash or sweeping a floor*)? If so, why do you feel that way?

3. This week, look for a task or responsibility you have previously ignored and take ownership in that area.

Key 9: Stay Focused

At the end of my college career, I had the pleasure of getting to know, and establishing as a leader in my life, a man known as Mr. C. He had found success at a relatively young age, was full of passion for his industry, and truly cared about people. I met Mr. C. through Mr. Tuna, whose story I told in an earlier chapter. I eventually began doing side jobs for him to help fund my way through college. I always enjoyed talking and sharing ideas with him. It was obvious he had my best interest at heart.

Mr. C. was in a different field of work than Mr. Tuna, and as I began working with him more, I became excited to learn a new trade under his leadership. As I learned the ins and outs of Mr. C.'s industry, I gradually developed a level of comfort. After working in the field for a while, I began to lose some of my excitement and drive. The grass began to look greener on the other side of the fence and, with that in mind, I started working after-hours and long weekends on other projects. I'm all for having side pursuits—you make a living from 9-5, but the majority of life happens outside those hours. However, I do warn against overextending oneself and losing all margin.

It was only a matter of time before I was completely distracted from my work with Mr. C. and was even putting more effort into my peripheral activities. Around this time, during a conversation with Mr. C., he pointed out something that, to this day, I believe to be valuable. He said, "Freedom, if you focused the combined energy you are expending in all these different pursuits in one direction, I can guarantee you would find success much faster."

Bottom line: He was instructing me to take a laser-focused approach rather than spinning multiple plates at once.

I decided to take his advice and invested all my energies in a singular focus. Sure enough, success was only a short distance away. Staying focused and allowing a leader to guide you is another step toward success.

Before I go on, let me be clear. Sometimes it will be necessary and wise to turn your focus outside the organization you are in or off the path you are on. I also want to clarify that being successful does not mean you can only do one thing in life. For most of us, it is necessary that we focus on several aspects of life—our jobs, our families, volunteer opportunities, etc. The important concept to grasp is to not engage in pursuing paths that compete with each another. Let me give an example.

The reason my extra endeavors became an issue was because I was still striving to succeed in my career, but then going home at night and focusing on business projects that I hoped would replace my day job. I quickly became exhausted and wasn't able to perform 100 percent on anything. My side projects nurtured a poor attitude regarding my day job, and my clients and co-workers were not impressed with my low energy level and lack of focus.

Another example would be when we allow ourselves to focus on things that are not the most important things *to us.* For instance, agreeing to help a friend with an intense softball league, when you are not interested in softball. The time and energy necessary to run the league will steal our time and rob our attention from our family and the goals we are pursuing. These are the types of decisions we need to consciously make.

The reality is that if we don't choose to be focused, we are actually making the choice to *not* be focused.

If you have ever spent time with middle school students, you know that boys in this period of life are boundless, amazing creatures. They're fast, tireless, creative, and often stinky. There is also another trait they are known for: having no focus! As a father of four, and someone who volunteers in a ministry for middle and high school students, I've come to think fondly of teenagers as being like golden retrievers. It feels like you have to run them for the equivalent of five miles in order to calm them enough to give you 15 to 30 seconds of concentration. Some days it feels easier to nail Jell-o to a wall than to have a focused conversation with a middle school boy.

With this in mind, consider what it takes to lead them to a desired destination. There is constant herding. It is exhausting, and at times disheartening, to attempt to guide middle schoolers in a specific direction, spending more energy redirecting than actually leading. Now consider that this might be what it feels like to lead unfocused adults as well.

I wish I could tell you that I am a laser-focused individual, but it's not true. However, I have learned some great lessons along the way about choosing where to put my attention, and I'm glad you get to learn from my mistakes on this one.

Recently, I was looking for someone to follow in the arena of online industry. I quickly discovered Pat Flynn, the genius behind the website, blog, and podcast *Smart Passive Income.* When I saw that he has proven himself to be successful and also spends time caring for his audience, I decided to follow him. Flynn is well known in his circles for a principle he calls the "be everywhere" strategy. As I listened to him describe this approach of using all possible channels of marketing to reach your audience, I initially thought, "This guy lacks focus!" He blogs, hosts a podcast, uses email marketing, utilizes Periscope and YouTube, and the list goes on and on. Over time, I realized that Flynn is, in fact, hyper-focused. His goal is to produce the most helpful material he can to benefit his Followers. The outlets he utilizes are not a lack of organization; rather, they are used with pinpoint accuracy to get his valuable content out to those who desire it.

Part of being a successful Follower is recognizing when you lack focus. Being very busy is not the equivalent of being productive. If you wish to stay focused, there are a few questions you should answer before moving forward.

What are your main goals in life?

If you don't know where you are going, you will not know where to focus or even if you have already arrived. In order to use GPS on a trip, you must know your next destination. Without a destination, you will never know if you are off course and out of focus.

Do you have margins?

When setting up a document or a writing project, one of the first things you do is set your page margins. This helps you to see the outlines of the page and leaves room for notes, blank space, etc. It is wise to leave room in one's life for rest and reflection. If you don't have time and space mapped out in your life, with clear boundaries in mind, it may be time to narrow your focus.

Is your leader focused?

The most obvious fallout of an unfocused leader is they will be incapable of leading you in a focused manner. As a Follower, you may have the ability to help your leader focus and move the whole organization toward its goals. High-capacity Followers have done this before! In the end, you are not in direct control of your leader's actions. However, you do get to choose who you follow so be aware of the direction your leader is headed.

Every time I think about the power locked within each of us as Followers, I feel excited and energized!

You are fully capable of changing your town, school, work place, church, home, and even the world. A God who loves you and believes in your great potential created you. If you're not a natural born leader, that's okay! You don't have to be in charge to make a difference, and a simple thing like focus will help you along the way.

Questions and Challenge to Unlock

1. Would you consider yourself to be a focused or unfocused person?

2. If you are a focused person, can you identify an opportunity to use your gift to benefit a leader you are following?

3. If you are an unfocused person, write a list of the items and side projects you currently have in the works or spinning in your mind. Prioritize them. Identify the ones that should stay on the list and some that should be removed.

Key 10: Lean In to Community

As a kid, Halloween was one of my favorite times of year. A sanctioned evening of mischief is something that every teenager loves. For most, this season ends around 13 or 14 years old. Nevertheless, my friends and I took advantage of this annual opportunity to cause trouble late into our high school years. There was one particular year that our antics got wildly out of hand.

It was Halloween of my senior year, close to 10 p.m., and my friends and I were sitting around trying to figure out what to do. After shooting down a variety of ideas, we finally formulated a game that we all agreed would be an excellent adventure. With a lack of wisdom within our group at the time, we thought our plan sounded both fantastic and challenging. We broke into two teams and headed out the door for a pumpkin stealing contest.

My team was two female friends and myself. We piled into my car and headed into the small town, with a population of 7,000 people, in which we lived. Off we went, the three of us across the front bench seat, with our minds set on success. As we drove, we began to brainstorm where we could find a large amount of pumpkins in one place. Suddenly one of us remembered that outside of town, there was a pumpkin field where a farmer grew them in mass quantities. Perfect—with this plan, we were totally going to win!

As we rolled up alongside the field, we turned the headlights off and quietly parked the car. Crazed by the idea of winning in such a landslide fashion, we feverishly began packing pumpkins into the backseat of the car. Big ones, little ones, and lopsided ones—it didn't matter, as long as they were pumpkins! We packed the car full, laughing and giggling as we opened the trunk of the car to fill that as well.

Ten minutes into our drive back toward town, one of the girls on my team realized she had lost her I.D. Stunned, she speculated that it must have fallen out of her pocket in the field we had just ransacked. Oh boy. This was like throwing rocks at a guard dog and then needing to deliver mail to the front door. We turned the car around and headed back toward the field, nervous that we would be caught.

As we neared the field, we could see lights on inside the house on the property. Nobody was outside though, so we quietly went back into the field and used lighters as flashlights to search for the missing I.D. that would tie us back to the crime we had committed. Thankfully, we found it quickly and got back on our way down the road. We couldn't believe it. We had gotten away with it! We were pumpkin stealing geniuses!

This euphoria lasted for 15 minutes, until we saw a policeman driving toward us from the opposite direction. Our smiles faded as we began the self-talk of all guilty teenagers who see the authorities moving toward them, "We're okay. Not a big deal. They're not looking for us." But as the patrol car passed us, I looked in the side view mirror and saw exactly what we had hoped not to see: brake lights.

As I pushed the gas pedal to the floor and fled down the street, I said, "Hold on, we're out of here!" As I looked for somewhere to hide, my mind was full of questions like, "How am I going to explain a car full of pumpkins? How did he *know* my car is full of stolen pumpkins?" I hit the brakes and took a hard left onto a dark side street. Thinking fast, I pulled into a driveway that was hidden from view by a large bush and slammed the car into park. There was just one last thing I needed to do!

With haste, I tried to shuffle the middle passenger into the driver's seat. As I was climbing over her, the four of our legs tangled up, I saw police lights behind us. As my friends spit out questions as to what I was doing, the only response I had was, "I don't have a driver's license!" As my butt hit the middle seat and my friend had been successfully shoved to the driver's seat, our legs still partially intertwined, she responded in a panicked voice, "Neither do I!"

As you can imagine, we got in some real trouble that night. Looking back, I feel embarrassed to think about how stupidly I acted. That night was quite an adventure, and my friends and I still laugh about our lack of sensibility that evening.

You are probably wondering what on earth this story has to do with the Power of Following. That's a great question! There are two reasons I wanted to tell you this story. The first is that it is a depiction of a time in my life when I didn't have it together and I made poor choices. The other is that it is a fun story that usually makes people smile. As you engage with a community of Followers, there is power in being humble enough to share a stupid moment for the purpose of instructing others and brightening their day.

Every day, billions of people go to work. For the majority of us, we go because we *have* to, not because we *want* to go. There's a reason so many people fantasize about winning the lottery or strategize how to retire early. I'm not saying we want to sit around and do nothing, but most of us would love the opportunity to do something else.

All four of my children are now old enough to have jobs. Some of them are pursuing their dream jobs while the younger ones are working after-school as a grocery cashier and frozen yogurt scooper. From the beginning, I have wanted my children to be aware of the fact that they hold the power to make or break a co-workers day. The opportunity of *having* to go somewhere every day, regardless of a desire to do so, is that you can become someone who is fun and can brighten the day of others who also don't want to be there. When you consistently live as a person who makes a point to brighten others' days, you will find that people seek you out. You'll become a magnet for other Followers and leaders.

The point I want to make is to be someone who is fun.

Be supportive of the other Followers and leaders around you. Be humble and occasionally tell stories of your failures. Be patient in listening to the stories others want to share with you. Don't be one of those people who do all the talking and none of the listening.

Being an individual who leans into the strengths and weaknesses of others is a pivotal skill for all Followers. We all know of examples, whether from real life or the movies, that show how investing in community makes a huge difference. Most of us are familiar with the 1993 film *Rudy*, which tells the story of football player Rudy Ruettiger. This is a great movie based on a true story. Years ago, I met Ruettiger at a conference and was impressed by the way he leans into the people around him. While Hollywood did take a little poetic license with the facts, there are several points in his story that ring true.

All Ruettiger wanted was to be part of the Notre Dame football team. He was a passionate, driven Follower. His desire was not to lead the team; he just wanted to be a part of it. His work ethic during college was intense. In the movie version of his story, his teammates become upset with the way he gives 100 percent even in practice. However, he continues to give his all because he wants to push them to be better and to be ready for the games on the weekend. He suffers bumps, bruises, cuts, soreness, and disappointments, all for the sake of bettering the team and in hopes of playing some day. Eventually, Rudy finds himself on the field. This happens not because of skill or physical prowess, but because Rudy has proven his dedication to the team's success. He is a great example of how to be supportive to those around you.

Another example that I heard recently comes to mind. In the story, a volunteer who was part of a weekly ministry team came into some difficult circumstances. There were financial and health concerns that had become very taxing and a source of great stress. The leader of the volunteer team, attune to the volunteer's troubles, offered for the volunteer to take a break from her commitments within the ministry. The woman, while deeply touched by the concern her leader showed, responded in a way that I love. She said, "Why would I step back when the community I have in this volunteer team is what I need the most right now!"

Those who follow a leader within the context of community have the potential to go further faster and stay dedicated longer. The power we have as individuals to offer support and joy to the lives of others is incalculable. The challenge I give to you is to be someone who others in your community are drawn to be near. Be someone whose friends or co-followers are drawn to for support when they experience struggles.

You might be thinking to yourself that you're not wired to be supportive and fun. Maybe you think that if you are fun to be around, leaders may not take you seriously. Or maybe you feel tired and community sounds like work. You don't have to be the life of the party, but we were all designed to be in community and to build each other up rather than down.

Isolation is no place to live, and in time, it can bring even the greatest leaders and Followers to ruin.

The benefits of living outside oneself are endless. For those of you who this comes naturally for, I encourage you to continue extending your influence and to be patient with those who are standoffish or reserved toward community. For those of you who do not feel that it comes naturally to you to be supportive and fun, I would encourage you to get out of your own way. Nobody believes the world would be a better place without fun, smiles, and community. Help others have fun. Be supportive to those who have need. Be a Rudy.

Questions to Unlock

1. Take a moment and think of someone at your work, church, or in your family, who is known for being cheerful and fun. Why do you and others like to be around them?

2. Do you think that people who are supportive and fun to be around have more opportunities or advantages than those who are not?

3. What stands in your way of becoming a support to someone in your community?

Key 11: Don't Be Misled By the Pack

My family and I are fortunate to live on a sizeable piece of land in the hills of northeast Pennsylvania. I don't own a gun, but many of my friends do. Many of them enjoy target shooting, but are limited in the places they can do so. That's why, a few years ago, I built a gun range on my property.

Near the gun range, there is a pond that holds lots of wildlife. We frequently see fish, turtles, snakes, and birds in and near the water. Included in our menagerie of wildlife are two herons. These beautiful creatures are tall, lanky birds with large wingspans. They remind me of the portrayal of Howard Hughes' plane Hercules in the movie *The Aviator.*

One afternoon, my friends brought over some Civil War and World War II-era rifles. It was surreal to hold a rifle that my grandfather would have carried when he stormed Bastogne in 1944. It was so loud compared to the modern hunting rifles I am used to firing. As we gathered around the range, the six-foot targets at least 150 yards in the distance, we noticed one of the herons flying near the pond. Since it was not in proximity of the targets or concerned about the group of men gathered in the yard, we carried on with our activity.

As the bird was midflight, one of my friends fired the loudest gun we had in our arsenal. All of us guys felt the concussion of the discharge. Apparently so did the heron. As we watched, the startled bird curled up in a ball and began to fall from the sky. It was as though it thought it had been shot and was simply giving in to the bright lights. After falling for 30 to 40 feet, it suddenly realized it was not, in fact, knocking on death's door and launched itself back into flight. *Whoosh,* its wings went back into motion and it continued its journey toward the pond.

That poor, scared bird. To this day, I have never seen anything fall from the sky so fast without being touched by an outside force. If we ever have a chance to meet, I'd be happy to reenact this incident for you. Like the heron, I am also tall and a bit lanky, and my friends never let me tell this story without acting it out.

As Followers, it is incredible the outside forces we allow to affect our direction. If we are not careful, we can be led astray or even sent off-course. When you decide to be a high-capacity Follower—a person that will follow a leader toward a destination and be part of the possible success of a plan—you have to take the reigns. The truth is, not all of the Followers around you will be as devoted to the mission as you are and may try to convince you to slow down or even stop. Additionally, going along with the pack can hold you back by polluting your mind with their whining and tearing down of leaders.

Our world is full of people who like to whine, but don't do anything to change the circumstance in which they are dissatisfied. Unfortunately, many of us see this in our own workplaces. We constantly bump up against people who complain about their workplace—how things are done, the management structure, the compensation, and the list goes on and on. This type of mentality isn't isolated to professional environments. Many volunteer organizations and sports teams face the same challenge. Honestly, this attitude can crop up in any place where there is a leader and a group of Followers. There is a sad tendency for people who do not wish to lead to criticize and tear down those who are in control. It reminds me of the *Monday morning quarterback.* Merriam Webster defines this person as someone who "unfairly criticizes or questions the decisions and actions of other people after something has happened." Sound familiar?

When unhappy people constantly surround you, it can be easy to also become unhappy. Don't let this happen to you! This type of thinking breeds dissatisfaction and decreases your quality of life. Similar to the heron, many people stop flying because they are convinced they have been targeted by an outside source. Despite your surroundings and no matter the attitude of those around you, do not allow yourself to be less of the Follower you were created to be.

Don't allow yourself to believe that just because you are not the leader, that you are exempt from taking action.

There is nothing wrong with identifying things that can be improved within an organization. In fact, as a high-capacity Follower and someone who desires to make a difference, you should look for these opportunities. The difference is choosing to be someone who enacts change with a positive perspective versus being someone who spends time complaining with no solution or plan of action.

There is a story of a young boy who walked past the home of an old man every day on his way to school. Every morning, the man would sit on his porch with his dog lying at his feet. And every day, as the boy passed, he would hear the dog letting out an unpleasant moan. One day, he finally stopped and said to the old man, "Hey mister, what's the matter with your dog?" The old timer responded, "He's laying on a nail." Thinking about it for a moment, the boy inquired, "Then why doesn't he move?" To which the old man answered profoundly, "Because it doesn't hurt enough yet."

If you are uncomfortable or sense oncoming pain within your organization, and know it will not resolve without action, don't hesitate to move. I don't necessarily mean to pack your bags and head out. I do mean that you should do something about the issue other than joining the pack, whining but unwilling to get up.

For some of us, the pack we are surrounded by may not have lofty goals to make a difference in the world. Although they are not actively whining about all that is wrong, they may be happy to sit back and meet the status quo. This type of pack is easily identified when you begin to make positive differences for yourself and your company, and you hear them chattering behind your back—or maybe even to your face! They are the first in line to not only point out the negatives, but will tear down your dreams as well.

In order to avoid being a member of this pack, I think it is helpful to talk about where these feelings may come from. If we can look at the root of these emotions and actions, we can avoid being knocked off track. Let's take a look at a few:

Misguided Protection.

Sometimes the most vocal people in our lives are the ones that care about us the most. The difficulty is that often the most vocal people in our lives may also be misguided. As you venture to take a new path and follow a new leader, the pack may be full of concern for you. When people see you raising the bar and beginning to stretch, they may ask questions like, "But what if you fail?" or, "What if it's hard and you feel discouraged?" The truth is, you might fail. But let me ask you this: Is it better to live a life in motion, moving toward a dream, or to moan in pain as you lay on a nail because you're just not ready to move yet? It's good to be surrounded with people you trust who will listen to and guide you, but it's ultimately up to you to discern if they are protecting you from real dangers or simply have misguided fears.

Fear of change or abandonment.

Packs are comprised of people who are like-minded and have similar goals. I was recently listening to the podcast of a successful internet entrepreneur who runs a five million dollar business. In his interview, he talked about a day when he was contemplating how to expand his business to reach the 100 million dollar size. He realized that in order to do this, he would need to find some new friends and peers who already ran businesses of that magnitude. This in no way meant he needed to say goodbye to his old friends and never speak to them again. It did mean, though, that he was going to make time for a new pack as well. Healthy packs are excited to see a member of their crew grow and extend beyond their previous accomplishments. Sadly though, this is not always the experience. As you stretch and seek to achieve more, it is good to be aware that your old friends might have feelings of abandonment or fear a shift in your relationship. If you have the courage to step out and dream big, don't let the pack hold you back from unlocking the ambition you have been given.

Low self-esteem.

Low self-esteem is the saddest reason members of the pack may try to hold you back, but it no doubt exists. There will be people in your circle of influence who may try to hold you back not to protect you, and not because they fear losing your friendship, but simply because they don't want to see you succeed beyond their own willingness to change. Low self-esteem causes people to feel fragile, unable to stand the idea of someone believing they can answer *the call.* What I mean by *the call* is that little voice inside us that says we are capable of more, that we are valuable and one of a kind, and that we have something special in us that the world needs. You know exactly what I'm talking about—we've all heard it. We may not be grand visionaries or amazing leaders, but we have tremendous value. When someone with low self-esteem hears this voice, they cover it up with a list of reasons why they aren't good enough. They know they do this, and will do whatever they can to keep others from answering it as well.

There is a passage in the New Testament that says, "And Jesus said to them, 'Follow me, and leave the dead to bury their own dead'" (Matthew 8:22). There is wisdom in knowing when to walk away from a pack that is faltering due to their own fear, laziness, or another negative emotion. At the end of the day, you can't allow yourself to be misled, held back, or paralyzed by the pack.

One outcome of following a great leader is looking for opportunities to better yourself and the people around you. If that continues to be your goal, those who decide to join you will be thankful. As the tide rises, so do all the ships in the harbor. You are that tide.

Questions and Challenge to Unlock

1. Take a moment to reflect and be honest with yourself. When you see a problem, do you talk about it with hopes of finding a solution or do you vent simply to just complain?

2. If you struggle with complaining, challenge yourself to alter the habit this week. Can you do it?

3. Is there someone in your life who speaks out of love and care, but seems to hold you back from breaking out and striving for higher heights? Who is someone you should seek to form a new pack with, in order to move forward?

Key 12: Watch Out!
Someone May Be Following You

Several years ago, my family began to attend the church we are still a part of today. One of the things that drew us to the church was that they had a great family ministry department. As we became more invested, we learned that part of their strategy is for attendees to not only show up on Sunday, but to also be a part of the volunteer "crew" that makes things happen week after week.

My wife Kelly, grateful for the way volunteers poured into our kids, decided she would like to volunteer in the childrens ministry area. Kelly began volunteering side by side with a woman named Jackie who was following the lead of the family ministries staff. Jackie was a Follower who wanted to make an impact and my wife followed her lead as she learned the ins and outs of working with kids.

Years later, Kelly began to invest in a little bit older group of students by leading the annual bus trip to summer camp. As Kelly spent time with this group, she was an excellent Follower and was always seeking advice from Jackie, as she was an overflowing source of knowledge and experience. For several years, the group of students who went to camp included Jackie's daughter Heidi.

When Heidi entered high school, she also began to volunteer in the student ministry at church. Low and behold, who was in her group when she began than none other than my daughter Annika! Heidi was an amazing small group leader for my daughter. On several occasions, she exhibited the cycle of following by seeking advice from her mom Jackie and my wife Kelly. At the time of this writing, Annika is in high school and, of course, volunteering at church. It thrills me to see her call or text Heidi for advice or seek the guidance of another leader in her life.

I love this story, not only because I love the people in it, but because it perfectly shows how even as you seek to become a great Follower, you too may be followed. All of the women in this story were volunteers and Followers. They were ultimately following the lead of the family pastor, but in the nitty-gritty, they turned to other Followers for input and support. As you reflect on this story, you observe a cycle of following that begins to take place, as the Follow*er* becomes the one who is follow*ed*.

This final Key to Following is huge. For many of us reading this book, we have identified that we aren't interested in being the leader. However, as the above story shows, a big part of being a Follower is leading other Followers in the process. I'm not trying to create a "gotcha!" moment in the last chapter, but the truth is that if you follow with excellence, you will end up being a leader of sorts.

There is no reason for you to be intimidated by the idea of leading others. Some of us have in our heads what a great leader should look like and we too quickly think, "That's not me!" Yet one of the amazing results of being a great Follower is that others will be compelled to follow you.

The Power of Following is that if you do it with excellence, you will become a leader without even trying.

Players become coaches and students become teachers. Consider names that we have come to associate with successful leadership; names like Robert Kiyosaki, Dave Ramsey, Andy Stanley, Tim Ferris, and John Maxwell. They are all followed by many, but even they follow others for wisdom.

Those of you who choose to follow a franchise system may end up the owners of restaurants and leaders of employees who buy in to your vision. Those of you who join the military and protect our borders may move up in rank, and other Followers will be honored to fall in behind you. Maybe you will decide to identify a leader to help you be a better man, woman, spouse, parent, or employee, and years from now will find yourself with the next generation looking to you for leadership. Being a dedicated Follower does not make you weak. Rather, it gives strength to those around you.

Challenges to Unlock

1. Sit down with a leader in your life and ask them who they follow. Ask how they came to the decision to follow that individual.

2. Identify someone who may be trying to follow you. Intentionally reach out this week and encourage them on a goal or project you see them chasing.

The No-Ribbon Wrap Up

I love how books are so structured. I've read many in my day—not as many as a lot of people, but enough to understand basic book structure when I see it. The endings of many books are quite similar. They take the storyline or content and wrap it up with a ribbon, tie it in a cute bow, and present it as a gift. A happy ending. Having read the ending, you can rest assure that all is well.

That is not the case for this book. All is not well—at least not yet.

The "yet" will be determined by how you decide to move. If you take action and chase your role as a Follower, the ribbon will be tied and the gift given. If you put this book down and decide to change nothing, then it's a "no-ribbon wrap up" for you.

This book was written with the hope that you will be the hero in the story. Yes, you! By identifying the change or a destination you would like to go, you become the hero in this tale. You have the opportunity to excel; not by becoming an amazing leader overnight, but by following someone who has the wisdom you don't yet have yourself.

You are the hero when you come alongside a visionary leader whose ideas can change the world when supported by a high-capacity Follower who will help make it happen. Without you, they may not accomplish their goal of making a difference. In order to make a difference, you must take the knowledge from these pages and apply it. Don't try to do all of it tomorrow. Start at the beginning and work through the keys bit by bit.

There is a story of a man who was hired to catch a lion who was eating the locals' livestock. They had tried over and over to catch it with traps and dart guns, but the lion always outsmarted them and got away. The hired hunter arrived on the scene and went to an area on the outskirts of town where lions had often been seen. On the first day, he put a pole in the ground with some food near it. Just one pole.

The next day, he went and the food was gone. He placed another pole several feet away, connected them with some fencing, and placed more food near the second pole. Two poles in two days. He repeated this process for days, slowly building a fence around the lion. On the final night, he went to look at where he had placed the food earlier that evening, and sure enough, there was the lion eating. He simply connected the final two poles and the lion was caught.

This is how change and achievement happen. We must place one pole at a time. If we move too quickly or in a scattered fashion, we will run out of energy, our goal will escape us, and we will give up. What we can do tomorrow is change one thing. Then after that one thing has been mastered, we can change another thing. Slowly, we can capture our dream one change at a time.

It's empowering to push oneself and to see accomplishment. It invokes courage to move forward.

Recently, I recruited my sons to dig a hole. We were in search of a pipe and needed to dig a hole four feet long by two feet wide by five feet deep. We weren't sure exactly where to find the pipe or if it was even there. After six hours of digging, the boys had reached four and a half feet deep and no pipe had been found. It was frustrating for them to put such backbreaking work into what may be a futile search. As you can imagine, their motivation was waning and it was becoming difficult to gather the strength to continue digging. Wiping sweat from his forehead, my son Evan reflected on how digging that hole mirrored many of our goals so similarly. As you take ownership of your life and follow a leader to a destination, there will be challenges. There will be times when you wonder if you will ever arrive. You may even wonder if you picked the right goal. You may even consider giving up. Don't.

At the end of the day, we found the pipe. My boys felt proud of their hard work. Their muscles were exhausted from the exercise and their minds were challenged with the temptation to give up which they had experienced. Their hearts had been lifted when the pipe was found and they discovered they were capable of pushing through to the end. That's what success looks like.

Here's a question for you: **Does it matter?**

Does it matter if you have an impact by leading or following with excellence? Does it matter if people are following you because you are a leader or because you are a high-capacity Follower? Does it matter if your goals have been achieved because you did it your way or by following someone else?

Does it matter?

The answer is *no*. It doesn't matter. While we may appreciate the tune and lyrics to "I did it my way," we don't have to buy in to the lie that if we don't do it alone and on our terms, then it doesn't count. Many times in my life, I've wanted to be the leader, and realized I wasn't equipped in that situation to lead. Despite my shortcomings, it didn't lessen my desire to be a better friend, husband, and father. I still wanted to be a leader at church, at work, and in my family. I had a decision to make. I could either chalk it up to "I wasn't born with that skill," or I could identify leaders to follow by asking questions, observing their actions, and soaking in their wisdom. I chose the latter.

As you still hold this book in your hands, I want you to ask yourself once again, "Who am I following and why?" You are following someone, whether you consciously decided to or not. Who are they?

When you take ownership of identifying a goal and a leader to follow, you have already set yourself apart from the masses. When you begin to choose the people you listen to and the books you read carefully, you will begin to absorb information and think differently. As you edify your leaders, follow with eagerness, and take ownership of your actions, you will begin to see differently. Finally, as you support and care for other Followers and your leaders, people will want to be around you and, yes, even want to follow you where you are going.

Now......

You have the Keys.

You are a great creation, designed for a purpose that no other person can fill.

You are the hero of this untold story.

Unleash yourself.

Go and follow.

Notes

The Andy Stanley Leadership Podcast. [Audio podcast]. Retrieved from http://itunes.apple.com

The Smart Passive Income Podcast with Pat Flynn. [Audio podcast]. Retrieved from http://itunes.apple.com

Tim Stanley. "Survey shows prisoners are kinder and more trustworthy than everyone else. Or so they think." The Telegraph, January 10th, 2014. Online News

Elbert Hubbard. "A Message to Garcia", The Philistine, February, 1899. Print

Scripture quotations are from the ESV® Bible (The Holy Bible, English Standard Version®), copyright © 2001 by Crossway, a publishing ministry of Good News Publishers. Used by permission. All rights reserved.